FIRST HERO IN OUTER SPACE

LAIKA
THE SPACE DOG

by JENI WITTROCK   illustrated by SHANNON TOTH

content consultant: Dr. Dave Williams, planetary scientist, National Space Science Data Center, NASA

PICTURE WINDOW BOOKS
a capstone imprint

Through the streets, alleyways, and markets of Moscow, a small, curly-tailed stray trotted warily. Every day, little Laika (LIKE-uh) rummaged for food and refuge for the night.

It was late summer, 1956. The Soviet Union prepared to launch *Sputnik*, the world's first satellite, into orbit. But street dogs like Laika knew nothing of outer space. What Laika wanted was food!

When a quiet man approached her, the little dog eyed him carefully. He held out a morsel of food in one hand. But what was in the other hand? Was this a friend?

Laika crept toward the treat—she could almost reach the meat! Then, *whoosh!* went the dogcatcher's net. Laika yipped! She struggled to get free, but it was no use. She was caught.

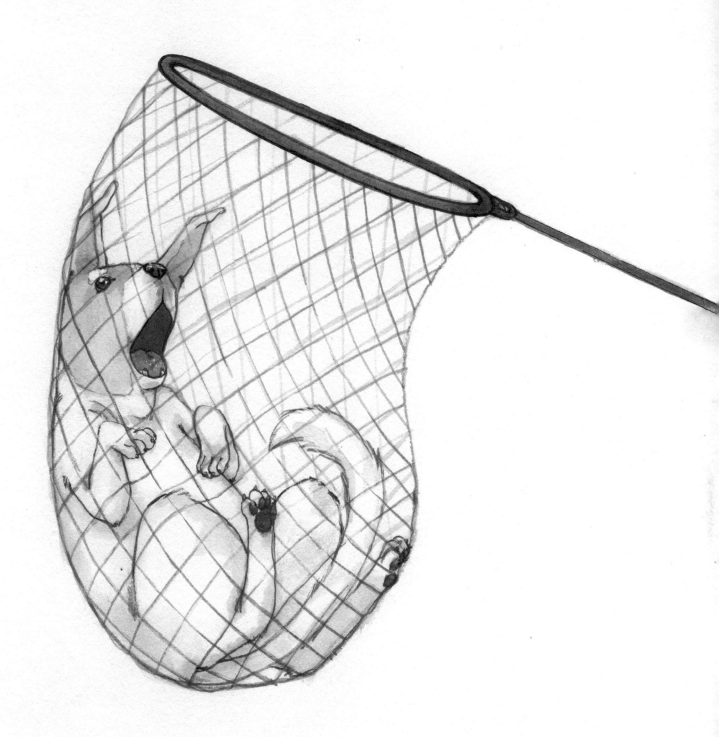

In a rumbling truck, the dogcatcher brought
Laika to the Institute of Aviation Medicine. This laboratory
housed street dogs to be used in scientific tests and missions.

While lab dogs were given food and shelter, they lost all freedom.
A hard road lay ahead for Laika.

Life as a lab dog was difficult. Machines tested how Laika handled extreme speed, pressure, vibration, and noise. Sometimes she was held in a tiny cage for days at a time. She learned to live in a very small space.

Dr. Oleg Gazenko and the trainers at the Institute liked Laika. She stayed calm and always did what they asked. The trainers called her *Kudryavka*, which is Russian for "Little Curly." She was nicknamed *Limonchik*, "Little Lemon," and *Zhuchka*, "Little Bug."

Soon Laika became one of three dogs considered for a special new mission. A second Soviet satellite, *Sputnik 2*, would be launched in less than a month. And this time, there would be a dog on board.

While Laika was finishing her training, *Sputnik 2* was quickly being built. No person or animal had orbited in outer space yet, and scientists were unsure if it was safe. Smaller rockets had flown dogs, mice, monkeys, and rabbits to high altitudes. But none had left Earth's atmosphere.

Laika saw other dogs leave for rocket test flights. Some of them never came back.

Scientists wanted to learn how space travel would affect an animal's body. A special space suit was made just for Laika. It would help her body adjust to changes in pressure. Machines would record Laika's heartbeat, blood pressure, and movements.

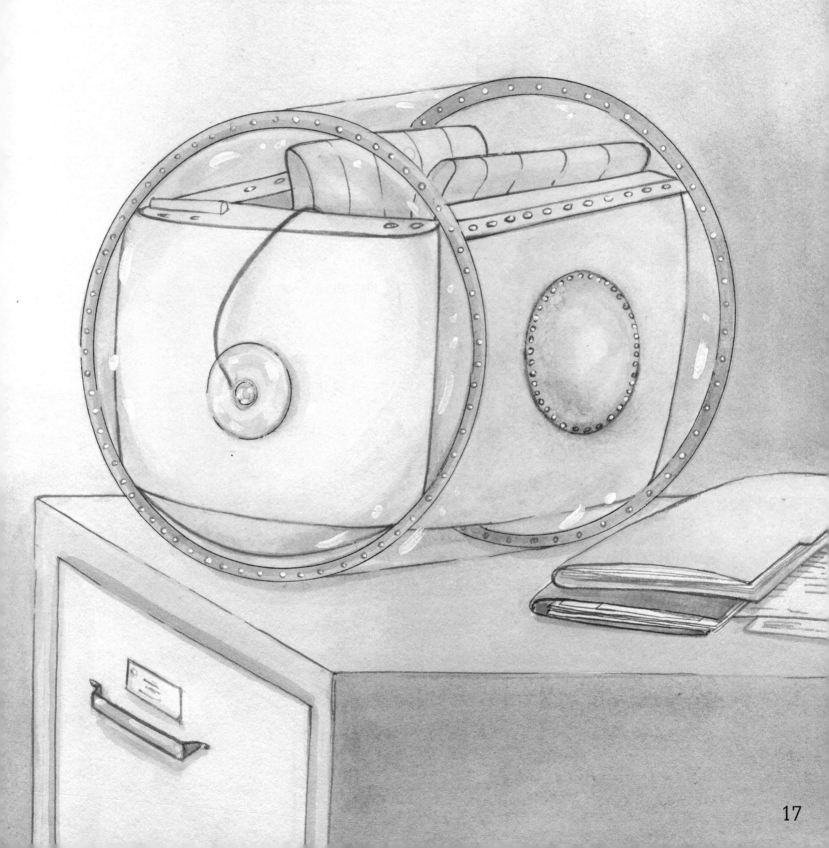

In late October, *Sputnik 2* was almost ready. A small cabin would be attached below the new satellite. It was just big enough for a small dog to sit, stand, and move around a little. A machine was added to dispense food.

On October 25, 1957, a radio report informed the world of Laika's daring mission. Laika had been chosen to travel to outer space in *Sputnik 2*. Soviet audiences listened as Laika barked into the microphone.

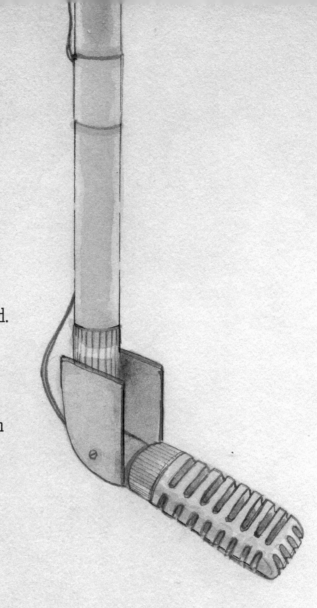

19

On October 31, 1957, Dr. Gazenko and the trainers suited up Laika one last time. Her handlers said a teary goodbye and wished their Little Curly the best of luck. Strapped inside her tiny cabin, Laika watched them walk away.

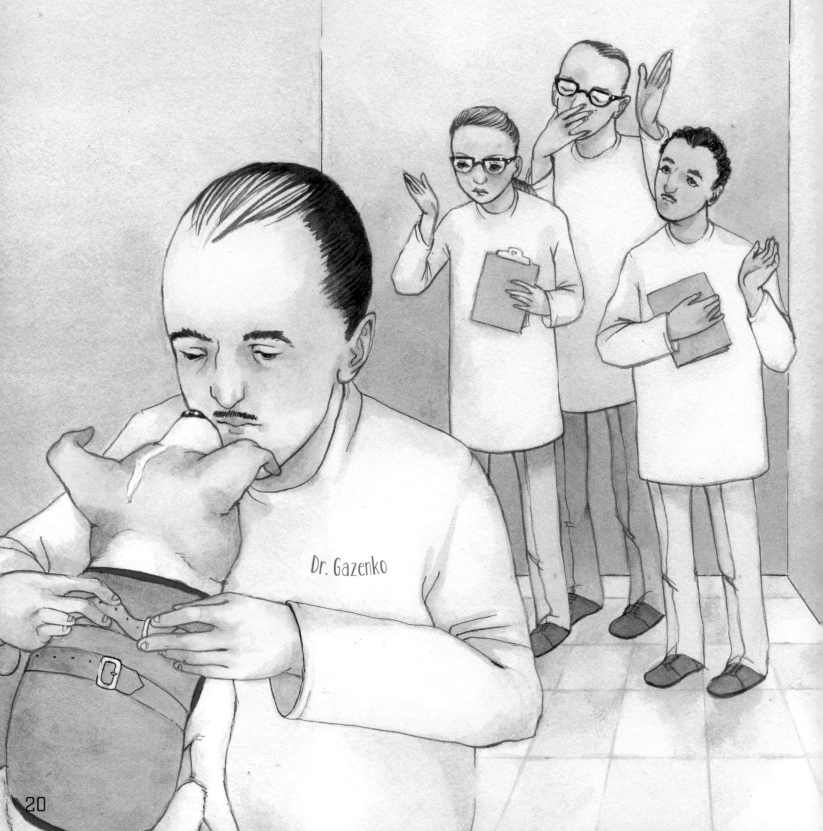

Laika waited alone in her little cabin. Finally she was transported to the launchpad and prepared for liftoff. Nearly four days passed before *Sputnik 2* was set to launch.

On November 3, 1957, the rocket's engines roared to life. The noise became loud, louder, then deafening. In a fiery blast, *Sputnik 2* lifted off the launchpad. Laika's heart pounded, and she barked in fear. The noise was almost unbearable. Even her training had not been like this. But there was no turning back.

A small crowd watched as the gleaming Soviet spacecraft sped up through the sky and out of sight. People across the Soviet Union cheered for one brave pup, the world's first true astronaut.

Scientists received the reports *Sputnik 2* sent down
to Earth. Laika's heart rate, blood pressure, and movements
showed she had completed her mission. A little stray the world
called "Laika" whirled around the planet at 18,000 miles
(28,968 kilometers) per hour.

A few hours into her flight, the cabin began to overheat. There
was nothing Laika could do. Her body gave in to heat and fright.
For Laika, the trip had ended.

But this tiny hero paved the way for many human astronauts to come.

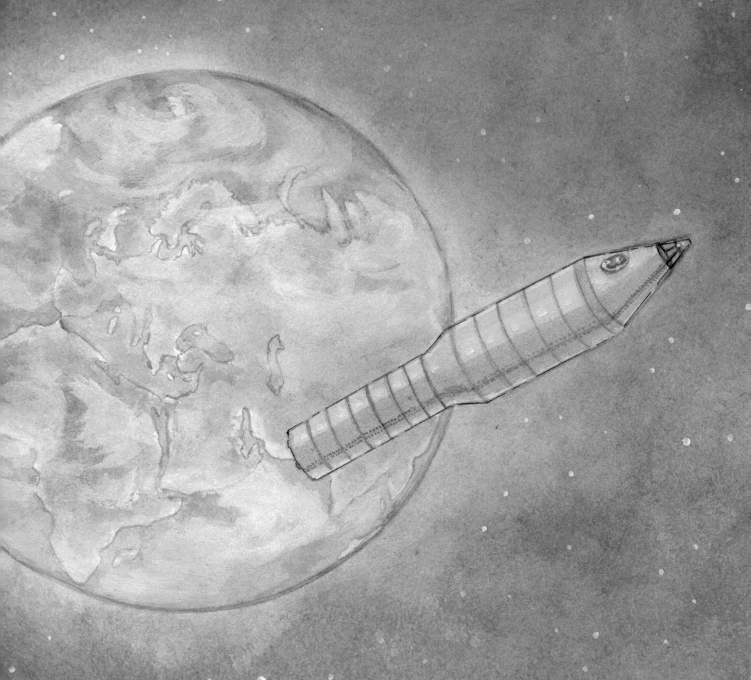

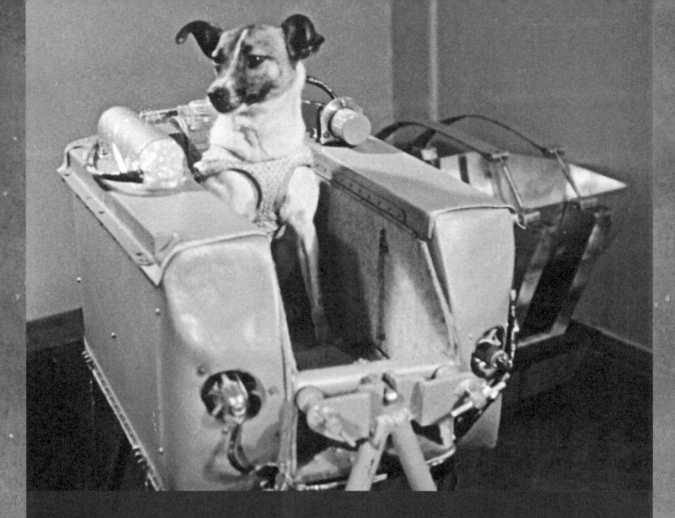

AFTERWORD

After Laika's death, *Sputnik 2* continued to orbit Earth for many months. Finally, on April 14, 1958, *Sputnik 2* reentered Earth's atmosphere. Catching fire, it fell back toward the earth. The satellite burned up before ever reaching land.

Thanks to Laika and many other animal heroes, space travel became a reality for humans less than five years later. In 1961, Russian Yuri Gagarin became the first person to launch into outer space. Oleg Gazenko, Laika's trainer, was one of the people who helped Gagarin prepare for his launch.

Laika was the only creature sent to outer space without a plan to safely return.

In 2007, exactly 50 years after her launch, a statue of Laika was unveiled in Moscow to honor her courage and sacrifice.

GLOSSARY

LABORATORY—a place where scientists do experiments and tests

LAUNCH—to send a rocket or spacecraft into space

LAUNCHPAD—a large area where a spacecraft is loaded and blasts off into space

ORBIT—to travel around an object in space; an orbit is also the path an object follows while circling an object in space.

SATELLITE—an object that moves around a planet or other cosmic body

READ MORE

Dunn, Joeming W. *Laika: the 1st Dog in Space*. Animals Making History. Edina, Minn.: Magic Wagon, 2012.

Hoena, Blake. *Stubby the Dog Soldier: World War I Hero*. Animal Heroes. North Mankato, Minn.: Picture Window Books, 2015.

Jefferis, David. *Race into Space*. New York: Crabtree Pub., 2007.

BEYOND THE STORY

The builders of *Sputnik 2* had to prepare the satellite in less than a month. If they had more time to work, how might things have turned out differently? How might it change Laika's story?

Sputnik's builders had to quickly complete the satellite in less than a month's time. If they had more time to work, how might things have turned out differently? How might it change Laika's story?

ABOUT THE AUTHOR

Jeni Wittrock is an author and editor of children's books and a lifelong animal lover. She attended Minnesota State University, Mankato, where she received a BA in English in 2002 and a MFA in Creative Writing in 2005. Jeni shares her Minneapolis home with her husband, Aaron, and a menagerie of beloved companion animals, including dogs, cats, and house rabbits.

ABOUT THE ILLUSTRATOR

Shannon Toth attended Sheridan College, where she received training in Interpretive Illustration. She worked as a freelance illustrator during her last year of school, after which she began working as a graphic designer for a Canadian clothing company. Eventually she returned to work as a fulltime illustrator. Shannon has held several exhibits around the world and has shown her work in Canada, the United States, and China. She has won several awards for ink illustrations and a children's book. Shannon currently works for a London, England based company, Illustration Ltd. She lives in Canada with her husband, daughter, and their two Boston terriers.

The author dedicates this book to Laika and all creatures, large and small,
who have lost their lives in the name of our safety and science.

Designer: Ashlee Suker
Art Director: Nathan Gassman
Production Specialist: Tori Abraham
The illustrations in this book were created with ink.

Picture Window Books are published by Capstone,
1710 Roe Crest Drive, North Mankato, Minnesota 56003
www.capstonepub.com

LIBRARY OF CONGRESS CATALOGING-IN-PUBLICATION DATA
Wittrock, Jeni, author.
Laika the Space Dog: First Hero in Outer Space / by Jeni Wittrock
pages cm.—(Nonfiction Picture Books. Animal Heroes)
Includes bibliographical references and index.
Summary: "Simple text and full-color illustrations describe the true story of Laika, the first dog in outer space"
—Provided by publisher.
Audience: 5-7. Audience: K to grade 3.
ISBN 978-1-4795-5463-8 (hardcover); ISBN 978-1-4795-5467-6 (paperback); ISBN 978-1-4795-5761-5 (paper over board);
ISBN 978-1-4795-5471-3 (ebook pdf)
1. Animal space flight—Juvenile literature. 2. Laika (Dog)—Juvenile literature. 3. Dogs as laboratory animals—Juvenile
literature. 4. Astronautics—Soviet Union—History—20th century—Juvenile literature. 5. Famous animals—Soviet Union—
Juvenile literature. I. Title.
TL793.W58 2014
929.43092'9—dc23   2014011380

Photo Credit: Newscom/RIA Nowosti/akg-images, 29

LOOK FOR ALL THE BOOKS IN THE SERIES:

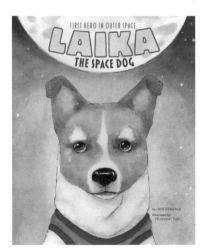

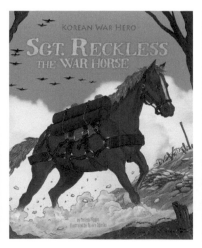
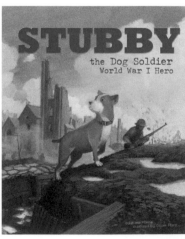

Printed in the United States   5863